GEO

K is for Keystone

A Pennsylvania Alphabet

Written by Kristen Kane and Illustrated by Laura Knorr

Sleeping Bear Press
310 North Main Street
Chelsea, MI 48118
www.sleepingbearpress.com

Sleeping Bear Press is an imprint of The Gale Group, Inc.

Printed and bound in Canada.

10 9 8 7 6 5 4 3 2 1

Library of Congress Cataloging-in-Publication Data
Kane, Kristen, 1969-
K is for keystone : a Pennsylvania alphabet / written by Kristen Kane ;
illustrated by Laura Knorr.
p. cm.
Summary: An alphabet book that introduces Pennsylvania's history, culture, and landscape, from the Amish of Lancaster to the Philadelphia Zoo.
ISBN 1-58536-104-6
1. Pennsylvania—Juvenile literature. 2. English language—Alphabet—Juvenile literature.
[1. Pennsylvania. 2. Alphabet.] I. Knorr, Laura, 1971- ill. II. Title.
F149.3 .K37 2003
974.8—dc21   2002014404

With love to Rob, Paul, and Dylan.
With heartfelt gratitude to Heather and Barb at Sleeping Bear Press.

KRISTEN

For Mom and Dad, Lavere and my husband, Mark.
You are each an inspiration.

LAURA

Lancaster, Pennsylvania, is home to a large group of Old Order Amish. Members of this close-knit community remain loyal to the traditions of their forefathers who immigrated to the area in the 1720s to escape religious persecution. Pennsylvania was a safe place for the Amish to settle, because William Penn planned his colony as a territory open to all faiths.

Remaining true to their beliefs, Old Order Amish are decidedly separate from the world. They reject vanity by dressing in simple clothing and are commonly referred to as "Plain People." They also shun the use of electricity and automobiles. Horse-drawn buggies are a common sight on Lancaster roads. Amish children attend school in a one-room schoolhouse until eighth grade. Their education continues at home, where family life fosters practical vocations such as farming, cooking, sewing, and carpentry. The Amish of Lancaster are renowned for their colorful handmade quilts and handcrafted wood furniture.

Pristine farms, one-room schoolhouses, and horse-drawn carriages reflect the legacy of this humble community.

A is for Amish,
   "Plain People" avoiding strife,
artisans, quilters, family folk,
      living a simple way of life.

Bill Cosby was born in Germantown, a town near Philadelphia. His lead role in the long-running television series (which he also conceived and produced), "The Cosby Show," made him one of America's dearest dads. Long before that hit show, he became the first African-American to star in a dramatic series on television. He won three of his five Emmy Awards for Best Actor for his role as a secret agent in "I Spy."

The "Cos" has also received multiple Grammy Awards for his comedy albums, and has written record-breaking bestsellers such as *Fatherhood* and *Time Flies*.

B b

B is for Bill Cosby,
Pennsylvania's famous son.
Author, entertainer, comedian—
many awards he has won.

Cc

C is for Caves and Coal mines,
tunnels of rock and "black gold."
Far beneath the surface,
Pennsylvania's heritage is told.

"Black gold" is a nickname for coal, a solid made from fossilized plants. This natural resource fired the industrial revolution in the United States. It was burned in homes, factories, and steam engines. Many people earned a living mining coal. Unfortunately, many coal miners also lost their lives in the mines, as it is a hazardous job to dig miles deep into the side of a mountain base where the coal can be found. Today, modern mining methods, safety training, and inspections have dramatically improved the industry's safety.

Coal isn't the only treasure to be found under Pennsylvania soil. Cave explorers will find amazing stalagmite and stalactite rock formations as they travel underground halls and rooms made from water erosion. Spelunking (cave exploring) and touring mines brings Pennsylvania history to life. Some of the many caves and mines accessible to visitors by foot or by boat include: Crystal Cave Park, Lost River Caverns, and Seldom Seen Tourist Coal Mine.

D is for whitetail Deer:
fawn, buck, and doe.
Through wooded hills and valleys,
gracefully they go.

The whitetail deer is our official state animal. Fawn (young deer), doe (female deer), and buck (male deer) thrive in Pennsylvania woodlands, but they can also be spotted grazing in fields. Early Native Americans and colonists relied on deer for food, clothing, and shelter. Today they are protected by state game laws. Sportsmen hunt deer during specified dates, keeping deer population under control.

As you travel about Pennsylvania, keep an eye out for these other state symbols: insect, the firefly; dog, the Great Dane; fish, the brook trout; bird, the ruffed grouse; flower, the mountain laurel; and tree, the hemlock.

Dd

E

E is for Easton,
a town where you can see,
the birthplace of crayons and markers,
in the Crayola FACTORY®.

The word Crayola® comes from the French word *craie* (chalk) and the first part of the word oleaginous (an oily paraffin wax).

In 1903 cousins Edwin Binney and C. Harold Smith created an overnight success with their Crayola® crayons made for school use. Seventy-five years later Crayola® markers were produced. Their factory in Easton includes a hands-on discovery center and offers demonstrations that show how crayons and markers are made.

Frank Lloyd Wright (1867-1959) is considered to be one of America's greatest architects. He believed buildings should be in harmony with their natural settings. Fallingwater, one of his most famous designs, is in harmony with the natural setting of western Pennsylvania's Laurel Highlands. Wright designed this summer home for the Edgar J. Kaufmann family of Pittsburgh. The millionaire department store owner and his family envisioned a home that would take advantage of the view of Bear Run waterfall. But Wright went a step further and integrated the waterfall into the design of the home. Fallingwater mimics rocky ledges as it hovers over, not beside, the waterfall. He designed this masterwork in 1935, and by 1939 the guesthouse was complete. The Kaufmann family was thrilled with their home and used it in every season.

Edgar Kaufmann Jr. entrusted Fallingwater to the Western Pennsylvania Conservancy in 1963, and its doors are now open to the public for guided tours.

F is for Fallingwater,
designed by Frank Lloyd Wright.
This house, built over a waterfall,
is quite a spectacular sight!

G is for Gettysburg,
a Civil War battleground.
President Lincoln delivered an Address here,
for which he is renowned.

On the first three days of July 1863, many thousands of soldiers lost their lives during the brutal Civil War Battle of Gettysburg. Pennsylvania's Governor Andrew Curtin was moved to create a proper burial ground there for the war dead. On November 19, 1863, at the dedication ceremonies of the Gettysburg National Cemetery, Edward Everett, the main speaker, gave a speech that lasted over two hours. President Abraham Lincoln was also invited to make remarks and delivered a most eloquent speech that honored those who had given their lives to save the Union. His speech, known as "The Gettysburg Address," gave meaning to the terrible battle and events that had taken place.

Later that day, Edward Everett commended Lincoln on his ability to say in two minutes what he himself had attempted to convey in two hours.

H h

$\mathbf{H}$ is for Harrisburg,
state government seat.
In this capital city,
Pennsylvania legislators meet.

Harrisburg is located on the Susquehanna
River in the southern part of Pennsylvania.
It was settled by John Harris, who built
a ferry and trading post there in 1719.
"Harris' Ferry" was later renamed
Harrisburg and eventually became the
state's capital in 1812.

The dome on Pennsylvania's beautiful
capitol building was modeled after
Saint Peter's Basilica in Rome.

Benjamin Franklin (1706-1790) is honored as one of our nation's founding fathers. The phrase, "An apple a day keeps the doctor away" was coined by him and was published in his *Poor Richard's Almanac*. But that's not the only writing Mr. Franklin left to his country. He played a key role in drafting the Declaration of Independence. His signature is on the Declaration of Independence, as well as the Constitution of the United States of America.

Ben Franklin's legacy also includes inventions, which made him a world-famous scientist. His bifocals replaced the need for two separate pairs of glasses. His lightning rod provided a path for lightning to follow to protect ships and dwellings. The Franklin Stove was an efficient heat source. This iron furnace could be placed in the center of a room to spread heat in all directions. Ben Franklin's most famous experiment was when he flew a kite with a metal key attached to the string during a rainstorm. He proved that lightning carries an electrical charge.

I is for the Inventions
of Ben Franklin, state diplomat.
Bifocals, a stove, and the lightning rod
are feathers in his hat.

Ii

J is for James Buchanan,
    our fifteenth president.
From an infant in a log cabin,
    to a White House resident.

J j

James Buchanan was the fifteenth president of the United States. He was born in a log cabin near Mercersburg on April 23, 1791. At the young age of sixteen, he was admitted to Dickinson College to study law, and later began a legal practice in Lancaster. He achieved tremendous success as a lawyer, and eventually became a member of the House of Representatives, a state senator, and the secretary of state before winning the presidency in 1857.

After serving as president, Buchanan returned to his country estate located in the quiet Lancaster countryside. Today, his beloved Wheatland is open for tours. Visitors will be charmed by the period interior of this Federal-style home.

Pennsylvania earned the nickname "Keystone State" because it was located in the center of the original thirteen colonies, similar to a keystone in the center of an arch. An arch will collapse without the wedge-shaped keystone in place.

It is fitting that it was called the Keystone State during colonial times because of its political importance. Pennsylvania was the meeting place for the colonies' Continental Congress, and Philadelphia, America's chief city at that time, was also the birthplace of independence.

K is for Keystone State,
Pennsylvania is said to be.
Like the center stone in an arch,
it was the central colony.

L¹

L is for Liberty Bell,
which made a patriotic ding
in historic Philadelphia,
proclaiming, "Let freedom ring!"

The Liberty Bell, a valued artifact of American history, is on display at the Liberty Bell Pavilion in Philadelphia.

Originally cast in 1752, it was cracked by the stroke of the clapper the first time it was rung, announcing the first public reading of the Declaration of Independence. The bell was recast and rung various times. Then in February 1846 the famous zigzag crack occurred while being tolled for George Washington's birthday. This crack was not repaired.

Today the bell is a popular tourist attraction. Visitors can read its inscribed verse, "And ye shall hallow the fiftieth year, and proclaim liberty throughout all the land unto all the Inhabitants thereof." (Leviticus XXV. 10)

Milton S. Hershey had to persevere in the candy making business before he would earn the title "Chocolate King." His first three attempts failed, but his determination led him to create milk chocolate to sell in America at a time when it was a Swiss luxury product.

Hershey's ambitions reached beyond the HERSHEY'S™ milk chocolate bar and chocolate products. He built a town with comfortable homes for his employees, as well as the ever-popular Hershey Park. Along with his wife, Catharine, he founded the Milton S. Hershey School, which nurtures more than 1,000 financially needy boys and girls. The Penn State Milton S. Hershey Medical Center is one of the leading teaching hospitals in the country.

Another important **M** that goes hand-in-hand with chocolate is Milk! Our General Assembly enacted milk as our state's official beverage on April 29, 1982.

m
M

E.CHOCOLATE AVE.

VE

M is for Milton Hershey,
the finest chocolatier around.
Crowned the "Chocolate King" in later years,
he created a Chocolate Town.

N is for Native Americans,
Original Peoples of this place.
Following a map of Pennsylvania,
their ancient past we trace.

The Delawares, as the Colonists referred to them, were the best-known Native Americans of Pennsylvania. The Delawares included mainly the Lenni Lenape (len'nee - len'ah-pay) and other groups that spoke a similar language. Lenni Lenape means the Real (or Original) People. They did, indeed, live in what was to become Pennsylvania before the Europeans arrived. William Penn had befriended them, but as time went on many descendants of Native Americans eventually relocated to Oklahoma due to land purchases, wars, emigration, and government-enforced relocation. The Lenni Lenape Historical Society Museum of Indian Culture in Allentown preserves Lenape culture and artifacts.

Other native peoples who lived in the area include the Shawnees, Susquehannocks, Iroquois, Senecas, and Eries. Names of regions and rivers in Pennsylvania call to mind the original dwellers of this land.

n
N

O is for Ore,
a rock with iron inside.
In Pittsburgh's giant steel mills,
molten iron was refined.

In the nineteenth century, Pittsburgh was our nation's largest industrial city. Located at the point of three converging rivers teeming with barges transporting raw material, Pittsburgh was poised to become the steel-making capital of the world. Pittsburgh steel mills manufactured steel for such American icons as the Brooklyn Bridge and the Empire State Building, and during the World Wars, produced steel, armor, and armaments in massive quantities.

Steel was also used to improve upon iron train rails. Andrew Carnegie began manufacturing stronger steel train rails in Pittsburgh. After merging with Henry Clay Frick's coke mining and processing company, our nation would soon see its first modern corporation.

The Rivers of Steel National Heritage Area, created by Congress in 1996, is dedicated to preserving the region's historic industrial saga and its remarkable renaissance.

O o

P is for Punxsutawney Phil,
seen at Gobbler's Knob.
Predicting the arrival of spring,
his shadow does the job.

Groundhog Day is February 2nd, which marks the midpoint between the beginning of winter and the beginning of spring. It is also known as Candlemas, a Christian feast day. Europeans believed that on this day, a hedgehog could predict the arrival of spring. German settlers brought this tradition to America. They watched for groundhogs (commonly seen in Pennsylvania) awakening in midwinter. If the groundhog saw his shadow, he would retreat to his den, which meant six more weeks of winter. If he did not see his shadow, he would stay awake for the arrival of spring.

The first official Groundhog Day was celebrated in 1887. Punxsutawney Phil, a now famous groundhog, is said to be over one hundred years old. His home is in the Punxsutawney Library, but he makes his annual prediction from a hole at the bottom of a simulated tree at Gobbler's Knob for all to see. This furry critter has earned his hometown the nickname, "Weather Capital of the World."

Q is for Quakers,
who found the right to choose,
under the leadership of William Penn,
their own beliefs and values.

William Penn is known as the founder of Pennsylvania. The name Pennsylvania means "Penn's Woods." It was named after William Penn's father, who was owed the land as payment for a debt from King Charles II of England.

Penn planned his colony to be a "Holy Experiment" which was godly and virtuous; a place where people of different races and religions would have equal rights. Upon arriving in the land granted to him by the king, Penn established peaceful relations with the Native Americans already living there. He purchased the land from them in the Treaty of Shackamaxon. William Penn is said to be the first great hero of American liberty.

Q q

Railroads are a rich part of Pennsylvania history, and they played a major role in connecting our young nation. The Appalachian Mountains were a daunting obstacle to westward expansion in the 1800s. A railroad line would have to cross the mountain chain, but building it would require an engineering feat. And that is just what Horseshoe Curve in Altoona is. Completed in 1854, the Curve provided a necessary gateway to the West. Railroads would now link cities and towns on opposite ends of our state, and eventually, of our country. The Pennsylvania Railroad became one of our nation's largest companies.

While Horseshoe Curve is still an operating line, many Pennsylvania railroads are no longer in use. Under the Pennsylvania Rails-to-Trails Act, abandoned rails are converted to hiking and biking paths. Following these rail trails is like stepping back in time as historic structures dot the Pennsylvania terrain. Train stations, bridges, tunnels, mills, factories, and canals nostalgically tell of what was once a thriving Pennsylvania industry. Over 80 former railroad lines are open to joggers, walkers, cyclists, cross-country skiers, horseback riders, and wheelchair recreation.

R is for Rails-to-Trails,
where mighty trains did run.
The lines are gone, but the paths remain
for hiking and biking fun.

S **S**

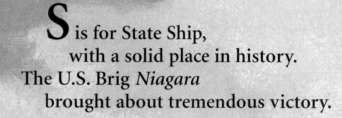

S is for State Ship,
   with a solid place in history.
The U.S. Brig *Niagara*
   brought about tremendous victory.

The *Niagara* was decisive in the defense of the Northwest Territory in the War of 1812. Under the command of Commodore Oliver Hazard Perry, it defeated a British squadron in the Battle of Lake Erie.

Over the years, the *Niagara* has undergone three reconstructions, which make its active day sailing program possible. When in port on Lake Erie, our state's flagship is open for guided tours. Within yards of the homeport is the beautiful Erie Maritime Museum.

Together, the *Niagara* and the Erie Maritime Museum promote education about the region's rich naval history.

T is for Titusville,
    the town where oil was found,
with the United States' first oil well,
    digging deep underground.

Titusville is located in northwestern Pennsylvania. It was near this town, at Oil Creek, that Colonel Edwin Drake struck oil. Drake, a former railroad conductor, used an old steam engine to power his drive pipe invention that drilled underground.

Onlookers jeered his attempts at first, but on August 27, 1859, Col. Drake met with success. His drill went deep enough to reach the seep oil.

Drake's oil well brought about the "age of illumination."

T t

U is for Underground Railroad,
though not a train to ride.
On a secret route to freedom,
Pennsylvania was a good place to hide.

In the mid-1800s a network of escape routes was developed to assist run-away slaves as they traveled north by the light of the North Star. Pennsylvania was an important state during this time because it bordered the Mason-Dixon Line, the official demarcation point between the North and the South.

Spies worked to return the escapees by patrolling routes to northern states and Canada, so African-American fugitives and the people who helped them began to use railroad terms as code words. Hiding places were called "stations." People who helped them to escape were called "conductors." Citizens in Pennsylvania, as well as the forests and mountain ridges of the state, provided protection for the "passengers" en route to freedom.

U u

V is for Valley Forge.
In a blustery cold December,
George Washington and his troops encamped.
Their valor we remember.

During the American Revolution, General George Washington chose Valley Forge as a strategic location to protect Congress while in session at York. Congress had formerly convened in Philadelphia, but British troops had invaded the city. The Continental army needed to protect Congress and the tenets of its recently drafted Declaration of Independence from further attacks. A lack of supplies and barren land at Valley Forge meant starvation and disease for weary soldiers, though: many men and women lost their lives that winter.

Nevertheless, it was at Valley Forge that Washington's army was reorganized under the authority of General Baron Von Steuben, and overcame the foe of low morale. Their perseverance and sacrifice during those six brutal months was a key determiner in the American War for Independence. Washington's army left Valley Forge with renewed strength to win the Revolutionary War.

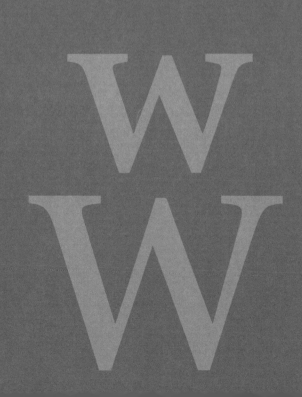

In the summer of 1939, Carl E. Stotz founded Little League Baseball in Williamsport. His neighborhood program quickly grew into a national sport. Today, children from many countries around the world participate in Little League Baseball. They strive to play in the Little League World Series, which takes place in Williamsport every August.

George W. Bush is the first Little League graduate to become president of the United States.

W is for Williamsport,
    where Little League began.
Giving children the chance to play baseball,
    was Carl E. Stotz's plan.

W
W

Founded by William Penn in 1682, Philadelphia is located in the south-eastern part of Pennsylvania along the Delaware River.

Penn designed the city as a place where people could live in freedom, under laws of their own making. He chose the Greek name "Philadelphia," which means "City of Brotherly Love," for his urban ideal.

Philadelphia was our nation's first capital (1790 to 1800). The first Continental Congress met in Carpenter's Hall in Philadelphia in 1774. Historic treasures such as the Liberty Bell, Independence Hall, and the home of colonial seamstress Betsy Ross are also located in this city. The same silver inkstand used by delegates to sign the Declaration of Independence and the Constitution remains in Independence Hall.

X marks the spot
on the map where you'll see
the "City of Brotherly Love,"
Pennsylvania's largest city.

Y is for Yellow and blue,
colors with statewide appeal,
waving proudly on the state flag,
bearing Pennsylvania's seal.

Y y

Pennsylvania's state flag depicts a coat of arms on a blue field that matches the blue of Old Glory. It is often knotted with a yellow fringe.

A ship, a plough, and sheaves of wheat form the state seal. These symbolize the importance of commerce, labor, perseverance, and agriculture to Pennsylvania's economy. An eagle (symbolizing the state's sovereignty) serves as the crest, and two black horses support the shield. An olive branch and a stalk of corn are crossed below the shield.

"Virtue, Liberty, and Independence" make up the state motto.

Our nation's first zoo, the Philadelphia Zoo, was founded in 1859 and opened on July 1, 1874. It contained a number of exotic plants and animals in its beginning, including the first male Indian rhinoceros exhibited in a United States zoo. It continues to draw crowds to this day with over 1,600 animals in residence.

The zoo's mission of conservation, education, research, and recreation is particularly apparent in the Primate Reserve, which opened in 1999. Visitors to this simulated timber mill-turned-conservation center will be entertained and enlightened as they encounter gorillas, lemurs, orangutans, and more. Our nation's first zoo is still a thrilling place to spend the day.

Zz

Z is for Zoo,
a fun place to spend the day.
The first one in the nation
was founded in Philadelphia, PA.

Of all the letters in this book,
choose your favorite one.
Look it up in the library
for more Pennsylvania fun!

A Key Quiz

1. What does the word "Pennsylvania" mean?

2. How did Pennsylvania get its name?

3. What is Pennsylvania's official state animal?

4. What makes Fallingwater different from other homes?

5. Who delivered a famous Civil War speech on Pennsylvania soil? What is the speech called?

6. Can you name Pennsylvania's state capital?

7. People call me one of our nation's founding fathers. I once flew a kite and discovered that lightning has an electrical charge. Who am I?

8. Pennsylvania's nickname is the "Keystone State." Can you find a keystone on the cover of this book?

9. How did Pennsylvania earn its nickname?

10. Who lived on the land we now know as Pennsylvania before the colonists arrived?

11. If you want to see our nation's first zoo, the Liberty Bell, and Independence Hall, where will you go?

12. What furry critter has earned a Pennsylvania town the nickname, "Weather Capital of the World"?

13. Why is Williamsport crowded with sports fans every August?

14. Why did William Penn choose the name "Philadelphia" for the city he designed?

15. What is Pennsylvania's state motto?

Answers

1. "Pennsylvania" means "Penn's Woods."

2. It was named after William Penn's father, who was owed the land as payment for a debt from King Charles II of England.

3. The whitetail deer is Pennsylvania's official state animal.

4. Fallingwater was built over a waterfall. World-famous architect, Frank Lloyd Wright, designed it.

5. Abraham Lincoln delivered "The Gettysburg Address."

6. Harrisburg is Pennsylvania's state capital.

7. Benjamin Franklin.

8. Two keystones are on the cover: one in the center of the arch and another on the front of the train.

9. Pennsylvania earned the name "Keystone State" because it was located in the center of the colonies, much like a keystone in an arch.

10. The Native Americans known as the Lenni Lenape or Delawares were the main original dwellers of Pennsylvania.

11. Philadelphia.

12. A groundhog named Punxsutawney Phil has made his hometown the "Weather Capital of the World."

13. The Little League World Series is held in Williamsport every summer.

14. William Penn chose the name "Philadelphia" because it means "City of Brotherly Love," which described his vision for the city.

15. Pennsylvania's state motto is "Virtue, Liberty, and Independence."

Kristen Kane

Kristen Kane is a native Pennsylvanian. She received a Bachelor of Science degree in Elementary Education from Penn State University where she served as Student Editor for the College of Education's student newsletter. Her years spent teaching in the classroom led her to create *K is for Keystone: A Pennsylvania Alphabet*. She wrote this book to introduce even the littlest learners to Pennsylvania's history, geography, and culture. Kristen has been published in the professional journal *Teaching K-8*, and has conducted educational workshops for elementary school teachers. She and her husband, their two sons, and their golden retriever make their home in Farmington, Pennsylvania.

Laura Knorr

Laura Knorr was born and raised in northeastern Pennsylvania and remarks "I may have left that delightful state but it is home in my heart wherever I may go."

She graduated with a Bachelor of Fine Arts degree in Illustration from Ringling School of Art and Design in Sarasota, Florida, and has worked as a freelance illustrator for a handful of years. Laura lives in Commerce, Georgia, with husband Mark, five fabulous kitties and a dog named Charlie.

K is for Keystone is her first children's book.